My Beautiful Colors
A REFUGEE STORY

by

Nyibol Bior

Drawings by Deng Paul, Fana McHugh, and Samantha Ferry

DORRANCE
PUBLISHING CO
EST. 1920
PITTSBURGH, PENNSYLVANIA 15238

Dorrance Publishing Co
585 Alpha Drive
Suite 103
Pittsburgh, PA 15238

Visit our website at www.dorrancebookstore.com

ISBN: 978-1-6470-2244-0
eISBN: 978-1-6470-2923-4

A rainbow represents both good and bad times.

After a heavy rain, beautiful colors appear from the sky, but people, trees, and homes may fall.

My journey as a child refugee was driven by both suffering and relieving experiences, like a flood after a heavy rain, followed by a beautiful rainbow. War was the storm. The chance to survive and be granted refugee asylum in the United States was my rainbow.

Today the color of my life is blue, but my goal is to live in the purple spectra, which I will soon describe. Blue is sometimes used to delineate a sad emotion. For example, after the war broke out in my country, the Sudan, I was detracted from all that I knew, from my village, and from my loving grandmother. I cried until I got a headache. I felt blue, but I survived the war and now I have the opportunity to grow out of the blue.

Blue does not have to mean sad. It can also mean "a new growth" or something refreshing to many. I spend most days working on achieving short goals in order to accomplish even longer goals, including the writing of my book about my experiences before and after the war.

I began writing in five different-colored pens about my journey and experience on this earth. The name of my book is *From War to PEACE*, and the colors on its cover are blue, red, green, black, and purple.

The opposite color of green is red. As a result of the Second Civil War of Sudan, which started in 1983 shortly after I was born, everything stopped except for the flow of refugees, their tears, and the oil across the continent of Africa; all the way from South Sudan to the delivery station in Khartoum, Sudan, on a pipeline built by men with money and skills.

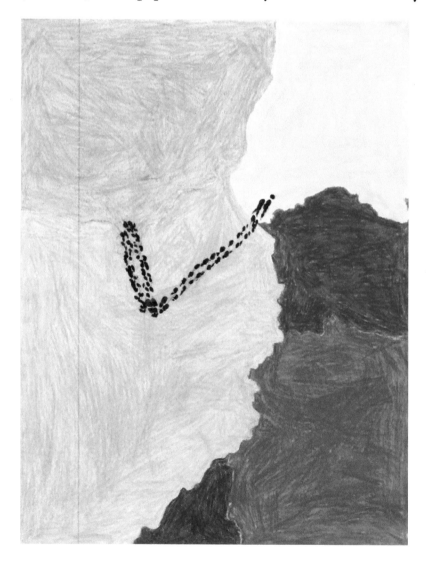

The villagers had knowledge about the earth, too, before the war. My grandmother took care of me and many of my cousins, cured diseases with her natural medical talent, and united all of us. Even though the men with money bought guns and waged wars, we had what money cannot buy. We had nature, friendships, and our love for one another.

When I was three, my grandmother cured me of migraines by surgically cutting the middle of my forehead with a razor. I still have my scar from the cut. I'm happy she did it because the mark reminds me of her and I no longer have excruciating headaches. Had my grandmother and I stayed together in the village long enough, I would have learned more about my surgery, and how she found medicine from the trees. Instead, the war destroyed my beautiful village and separated me from my grandmother.

For many years, the people in the villages refuse to fight, but war continually disrupts their peace.

Oil, minerals, and many other precious resources from the earth are what keep China and other countries in Africa and the world's eyes on both Sudan and South Sudan, but I think the most important resource we have is the water we drink from the Nile River. Without water, I would not be alive today. The fight for the need for oil has killed over two million people because the government doesn't know how to share it.

In 2011, South Sudan became the newest country in the world after seceding from Sudan due to many decades of war, but as an immigrant from Africa in the United States, I have accepted the world as my home. I claim the entire planet as my green home, but the people who wage wars and stir up hate turn my home into a violent red.

Red represents the bloodshed because of war, which breaks many hearts, including the heart of planet Earth. It is also the loneliness that follows, the lack of remorse, acts of terrorism, xenophobia and racism, including the bullying I encountered in schools and public places upon my arrival to three different countries. After the war broke out in Sudan, I walked to Ethiopia, a country nearby, but there was a coup and Ethiopia's new government decided to chase all refugees back to the warzone in Sudan. I crossed a river to return to my village, but the fighting became fierce, and for a long time, I did not have a place to call home. Since many bombs were being fired at civilians, I could not stay with my grandmother. I had to leave her for the second and the last time, and this time, I managed to walk to a refugee camp in Kenya, another country in Africa, where my family and I received refugee asylum. After walking over 1,000 miles, the United Nations finally gave my family and me a chance to start a new life in a different country.

In Kenya, there were police raids in homes of people like me who were waiting for a chance to relocate to developed countries. I can't imagine having been returned back to a warzone again while my family worked on the application to be moved to the United States. Also, students in Kenya made fun of me for being from a war-torn country, but I remained strong and made good grades in school by always being in the top ten percent of my class.

I moved to the United States with only love in my heart, and my refugee story to tell. I was in a lot of pain from my past and not everyone liked me because of my experience. I learned that some people decide to hate because they haven't learned how to love those who don't share the same experiences or talk or look like them. But not to worry, they will learn when my story reaches them.

Even though red can mean suffering, it can also stand for love, hope, and sacrifice. That is why the United States flag has red stripes. Red brought hope because my hurtful experiences encouraged me not to give up; they are all part of a new beginning. Red may be challenging, but it enables me to show unconditional love. It means I've gone through so much, yet remain very strong.

After any war, a country must learn and rebuild itself. My country, the Sudan, has not stopped fighting since the day I was born, and that's why I was given my new country, the United States, but something else happened. In school, I was bullied for being black. I've had to learn that what people think of me does not truly define who I am. All my colors are beautiful and they show up when I tell my refugee story.

Misinformed people can be ignorant because they have a lack of understanding. My job is to teach them why I was made black. It's simple, really. My country, South Sudan, has a very hot climate and its native people were made black so that when the sun hit their skin, their rich pigment protects them from burning. Sometimes people wonder why I don't get sunburns or wear sunscreen. This is because my skin is made to withstand the sun. The Sudanese people are black, and the country's name, "Sudan," means land of the blacks because most people in the **region** *have dark skin.*

I'm bound to do well within my profession as a teacher and human being. I will start by making sure children all over the world learn about my story and my beautiful colors.

Today, I use my time to volunteer and speak in libraries, and to little girls and boys in schools, just to let them know that their colors are beautiful, "being different" is a gift. Their red as in a traffic light must change to green. Life is supposed to be protected and lived. Most of nature is green, as in a growing land of maize with huge green leaves in my village, or a warm welcome into a foreign land, like the United States, where a green card is legally issued to migrants in search of a better life.

Green means GO! I stand for love, kindness, and freedom. Green is like the dream I had during a one-thousand-mile walk from my village to Ethiopia and then the Kakuma refugee camp in Kenya. I was barefoot, too. Thousands of people, mostly women, walked tirelessly through the path, with babies and luggage strapped to them. Among these people were my family and many relatives who were all forced out of their homes to endure pain and suffering in the wilderness. We walked for a few months, during a rainy season, and through the desert, hiding whenever we were informed of a nearby gun fight or bomb attack. I became very tired. I wanted everything to turn green.

While walking by a hill, I noticed beautiful houses. In that moment, I began to think, *Kawajat (white people) probably live there.* The walking path had hardened mud and small pieces of rocks. And when it rained, we sometimes slid and fell into mud pits. The hot yellow and orange sun cooked my bare feet and skull, while the rocks made it difficult to walk. My only wish within every step I took was to STOP and rest. I got onto my knees and felt the comfort of a resting place. Just like a tree cannot live without water, I was ready to give up because I was not growing. Then I heard my father's voice saying, "We're almost there, Bol, get up!" I got up slowly, and as I began to walk again, I fell asleep and had a dream. The pain disappeared from the moment my father's voice soothed me to sleep.

Suddenly, I was in one of the houses on the hill, accompanied by two married people, a man and a woman. They invited me in, had me sit in a chair, washed my tired feet, fed me with soup, and tucked me into bed as if I was their own child.

Soon the dream faded away but as I continued to walk, I had gained so much hope and strength. *That was my life in the green spectra, and my heart was full of greenery, the way the grass covers the ground after plentiful of sun and rain.* I was fed, loved, energized, and renewed after I woke up, like a beautiful flower. The dream reminds me that I have not only the right to live, but also the right to feel safe and loved as I look forward to a life in purple.

The color blue represents the journey, *From War to Peace,* and the process of leaving this world a better place. Living in America leaves me with the desire to assist in ending hunger in the world. America is a great country, one that has allowed me to follow my dreams and be free. I happen to live in a developed and peaceful place, which makes earth easier to live in. Blue is in the process of being just as good as green, but it takes persistence to get there. Poverty is that blue, sad emotion which can be altered for the sake of prosperity. This is the process of going From War to Peace, like I talk about in my book, *From War to Peace.*

My next color which I'll describe is purple, the color of reward. This is the miraculous state of life for me. Purple makes all colors beautiful. In America, a Purple Heart is awarded to those who have been killed or injured in a war.

There is hope and ambition in purple. It is also nurturing and comforting to the eye, body, and even soul. The reward I would like to receive is the completion of my book, *From War to Peace,* and leaving this world a better place for the forgotten. I want joy in my heart, and a closer relationship with God. We all have something to fight and it does not have to be each other. We can fight for the environment, against poverty, health problems, human trafficking, animal extinction, education deprivation, just to name a few among many issues threatening our planet. For now, my job is to tell my story, "From War to Peace," so that people can see all the ways in which my life has changed its colors. For now, I am dreaming and living a blue and comfortable life.

Epilogue

The first color in which I began writing my book is black, and so was the earth before the sun, moon, and stars came to be. I was struck by my experience as a dark-skinned person from Sudan who got bullied in school by people of color for being too dark. I decided I'd have a chapter in my book called "My Beautiful Colors," now a book of its own because it didn't fit into the narrative well. I began writing in different colors in a school I was working in as a substitute teacher in 2007. I decided I'd spend my planning and lunchtime writing this chapter after a group of students at the high school where I worked saw me and proceeded to laugh at me in the hallway for being extremely black. All the memories of bad experiences after the war returned and instead of continuing my refugee story, I began to contemplate a way to inspire the world to love my skin color and help ensure children with dark skin don't go home crying every day because other children are ashamed of them for being different. The fact is, we're all human and that's all that should matter.

Black is the color which absorbs light, as the dictionary describes it. In my own words, black makes room for light. Without dark or black ink, the words in this book would not be able to appear on this white paper. The night leaves room for the day, and when babies are born, they don't expect to be called black, brown, or white. The baby is human first and expects to be called by their given name. After the baby gets its name and grows, it learns that he or she is black, brown, or white because that is what society teaches them. It then learns that the lighter the human the better, or the darker the human the worst, but black is not evil even though many world religions associate it with evil. It's just the color of one's skin, not the color of one's soul, as in mean spirited.

In middle school, African-American students were curious to know why I was so dark, and their goal was to make me feel that black is the most atrocious skin color on the planet. I wondered why their race is black but to them my black was ugly. They said I'm black like charcoal, that I've been in the oven for too long. Sometimes they called me purple, which I loved except for other bad names, like burnt toast. It helped when I couldn't understand what they were saying because my English was still limited. If black were evil, then I would be evil but I think I'm pure. My skin is as dark as the night sky and everyone who loves me for who I am are like the stars in my world, my rainbow, and my beautiful colors. I believe I'm beautiful and my skin is radiant within its darkened complexion.

If I were evil, then I would try to end the world despite its cruelty toward my presence in it, but I choose to teach about how black is beautiful. Black is the color in which my book *From War to Peace* will be read in. Many Sudanese have used skin-bleaching creams because just like I was tired of the war and felt on my knees, some of them are tired of being made fun of for being black. I'd like to help change the negative scripts people and the media write about dark skin, by simply loving and helping others realize that their God-given potentials do not have to be defined by a color and that black deserves to exist, to be praised and loved just like my future autobiography, *From War to Peace.*

Acknowledgment

As a first-time author, the completion of this excerpt of my refugee story was not an easy or inexpensive task. I would like to thank everyone who has helped in some way. To my friend Leah Bassoff, the author of "Lost Girl Found," thank you for editing and suggesting that "My Beautiful Colors" be written as a children's book. Keep changing the world through your desire to help others with no expectations except making the world a better place for all. I would like to thank the following Colorado public organizations for giving me the opportunity to tell my refugee story: The Raven Narratives, Carbon Valley Branch Library, Dolores Public Library, Silt Branch Library, the Carbondale Branch Library, Dolores High School, Longmont High School, Roaring Fork High School, and Summit Bound Church. To all the organizations, including Summit Bound Church, Sarah and Tom at the Raven Narratives, friends, and family who have donated money to help me pay for this project, I will make sure your gift is multiplied. This book was not easy to illustrate and it would have been nearly impossible for me to come up with the art alone. Artists, Deng Paul, and Samantha Ferry did their best to depict my journey and dreams along the way. Maureen Rothman, thank you for using your PDF editor to type the title. Denise Wright, for reaching out to me to speak at Roaring Fork High and arranging to have your students and I collaborate to have the cover and Spanish translations done. Finally, I would like to thank the 9th grade team at Longmont High School, including Carly Jiron, Courtney Campbell, Kerri Courtney, and John Fuller, for their continuous efforts to help their students realize their potential by simply using stories like mine to help inspire them. I have done my best not to forget anyone, but if I did, please take my endless and continuous efforts to share my story as my way of showing how grateful I am for your love and support.

CPSIA information can be obtained
at www.ICGtesting.com
Printed in the USA
BVHW052200230421
605093BV00003B/17